The Conflict Resolution Library™

# Dealing with Tattling

• Don Middleton •

The Rosen Publishing Group's
**PowerKids Press**™
New York

This book is dedicated to my wife, Sue; my daughters, Jody and Kim; my mother-in-law, Mimi; and my parents, Bernice and Helmut Bischoff. Also, special thanks to authors and friends Diana Star Helmer and Tom Owens for believing in me. —Don Middleton

Published in 1999 by The Rosen Publishing Group, Inc.
29 East 21st Street, New York, NY 10010

Photo Credits and Photo Illustrations: pp. 4, 8, 16, 19 by Seth Dinnerman; p. 7 © Mark Bolster/International Stock; p. 11 © Noble Stock/International Stock; p. 12 by Maria Moreno; p. 15 © Dusty Willison/International Stock; p. 20 by Guillermina de Ferrari.

First Edition

Layout and design: Erin McKenna

Middleton, Don.
  Dealing with tattling/by Don Middleton.
    p.     cm—(The conflict resolution library)
  Includes index.
  Summary: Explains what tattling is, why people do it, and what the consequences might be; then suggests alternatives to this behavior and ways to resolve problems created by talebearing.
  ISBN  0-8239-5266-5
  [1. Talebearing in children—Juvenile literature. 2. Interpersonal relations in children—Juvenile literature.
  [1. Talebearing. 2. Interpersonal relations.]  I. Title.  II. Series.
BF723.T3M3   1998
302.3 4083—dc21
                                                            98-22632
                                                                CIP
                                                                AC

Manufactured in the United States of America

# Contents

# Tattling

Tattling is when you tell another person's secrets to get that person in trouble. A classmate might tell your teacher you didn't finish all of your homework. Your younger brother may have told your mother you didn't make your bed. When **siblings** (SIB-lingz) tattle on one another, it can cause family arguments. Tattling isn't just telling the truth. Tattling is telling on other people so that they will get in trouble.

▼ Tattling on siblings can lead to hurt feelings.

# Helping One Another

You probably like to hang out with your good friends. You might share how you feel about certain things and look out for each other. Good friends don't tattle on each other. Instead, a good friend will try to warn you before you make a mistake. Or you might remind your friend when she forgets to do something she was supposed to do. Part of being a good friend is remembering what's important to your friend. By doing this, you can help her make better choices.

*Good friends help each other, not hurt each other.* ▼

# A Computer Tale

Computer class was almost over.

"Before you go," said Mr. Gidzak, "be sure your computer is shut down properly."

"I'm done and I'm outta here!" Jill said.

Jill's friend Sue shut down her computer and got up. Just then, she noticed Jill had accidentally left her computer on. Sue knew Jill didn't mean to do this. But if Mr. Gidzak found out, Jill would get in trouble. Instead of tattling on her, Sue turned off the computer for Jill. Helping people is a better **solution** (suh-LOO-shun) than tattling.

▼ It's nice to help out friends if they make a simple mistake.

# Feeling Ignored

Sometimes people feel ignored or left out. Maybe you feel that your mother spends more time with your little brother than she does with you. When a person feels ignored, he may feel like no one cares about him. If you ever feel this way, you may tattle to get attention. But tattling will only get you the wrong kind of attention—hurt feelings and angry words. Instead, talk to others about your feelings. Seeing that they care will let you know you're not alone.

Tattling on someone when you feel bad will only make you feel worse. ▼

# Doing What Is Right

Everybody has to deal with tough questions about what is right and what is wrong. What if you are the only student to see another steal money? Maybe there is an older student bullying younger kids. Or what if you find out your teenage brother has been drinking? It may be hard to see the difference between tattling and telling the truth. But telling the truth is the right thing to do when people are hurting themselves or others. When things like this happen, telling the truth isn't tattling.

▼ *Telling the truth might make someone angry, but it might help a person who is hurting himself.*

# The Weapon

Kenny and Jeff were talking about the school bully.

"Why do we let him get away with bullying?" asked Kenny.

"What if he really hurts someone?" Jeff wondered.

"He told some of the other kids that he carries a knife," Kenny said.

Kenny knew he needed to tell the principal.

The principal said, "I will look into this."

Kenny knew he'd done the right thing.

Sometimes *it's hard to tell the truth, but it's important to do it if it helps others.* ▼

# Trying to Hurt

Even though you may get along with most people, there may be some kids you don't get along with. You always seem to be fighting or teasing each other. If you hear a secret about them or if you know something they did wrong, you might be tempted to tattle on them. After all, you know it would get them in trouble. But you have to ask yourself if you're telling the truth about something they're doing that's hurting them, or if you're just tattling. If you're just tattling, it's best not to say anything.

▶ *There may be some kids that are hard to get along with, but tattling on them might make things worse.*

# Telling the Whole Truth

Sometimes you can be called a tattletale for telling the truth. Maybe your mother called from work and asked if your sister walked the dog. You told her she didn't and your sister got in trouble. Maybe a teacher asked who was playing in the gym after school. You told the truth and your friends got **detention** (dih-TEN-shun). If someone asks you a question, you shouldn't lie to cover up. You are telling the truth, not tattling. Owning up to something you did wrong is hard. You may have to face tough **consequences** (KON-suh-kwen-siz).

18

*Accepting tough consequences is part of growing up and learning from your mistakes.* ▶

# Protecting Yourself from Tattlers

Each of us makes mistakes or forgets to do certain things. But when another person notices, he may tattle on you. There are different ways to handle this. You could get mad at the person, but that might only make the problem bigger. It's better to admit you were wrong. Telling the other person you are sorry for what you did helps. You can ask the tattler to come to you first the next time, so you can have a chance to fix the problem. Kids and adults will **respect** (rih-SPEKT) you for that.

▼ *Talking out a problem makes you and the tattler respect each other.*

# Turning Yourself In

Scott and Gerry were throwing a football around during lunch.

"Here, catch one more pass," Scott said. The ball hit a window and cracked it.

"What do we do now?" asked Gerry.

"I did it. I'm going to have to pay for it," Scott said.

Even though they were scared, Scott and Gerry walked to the office. They wouldn't have to worry about anyone tattling on them. Scott and Gerry were owning up to what they did and telling the truth.

# Glossary

**consequence** (KON-suh-kwens) Something that happens in response to something you did.

**detention** (dih-TEN-shun) When you are kept after school as punishment.

**respect** (rih-SPEKT) Admiration and approval.

**sibling** (SIB-ling) A brother or sister.

**solution** (suh-LOO-shun) An answer to a problem.

# Index